I am...
We are...

Copyright © 2019 by Sandra Higgins.

All rights reserved.
No part of this publication may be reproduced, distributed, or transmitted in any form or by any means,
including photocopying, recording, or other electronic or mechanical methods,
without the prior written permission of the copyright holder,
except in the case of brief quotations embodied in critical reviews and certain
other noncommercial uses permitted by copyright law.
For permission requests, write to the publisher, addressed
"Attention: Permissions Coordinator," at the address below.

Soft Cover ISBN: 978-1-64318-040-3

Hard Cover ISBN: 978-1-64318-041-0

Imperium Publishing
1097 N. 400th Rd
Baldwin City, KS, 66006

www.imperiumpublishing.com

I am...

We are...

WRITTEN & ILLUSTRATED
BY SANDRA HIGGINS

Dedication

This book is dedicated to all my grandchildren:
Kaylee, Sydney, Riley, Rachel, Jon, Sarah, Adam, Molly, Josie, Emmett, Mariah, Regan, and Maddox.

My great-grandchildren: Berkley, Ava, Finn, and Eli.

May they always see the beauty in colors.

I am **black**

I am white

I am yellow

But we are all cats

I am blue

I am red

I am yellow

But we are all birds

I am grey

I am **brown**

I am white

But we are all dogs

I am **black**

I am white

I am **brown**

But we are all people

www.ingramcontent.com/pod-product-compliance
Lightning Source LLC
Chambersburg PA
CBHW061152070526
44584CB00034B/4490